![Disney Learning]

WONDERFUL WORLD OF
DINOSAURS

As a 2008 Milken Educator, I take the challenge of reviewing educational materials seriously. As I examined the Disney Learning series, I was impressed by the vivid graphics, captivating content, and introductory humor provided by the various Disney characters. But I decided I should take the material to the true experts, my third grade students, and listen to what they had to say. In their words, "The series is interesting. The books are really fun and eye-catching! They make me want to learn more. I can't wait until the books are in the bookstore!" They looked forward to receiving a new book from the series with as much anticipation as a birthday present or a holiday gift. Based on their expert opinion, this series will be a part of my classroom library. I may even purchase two sets to meet their demand.

Barbara Black
2008 Milken Educator
National Board Certified Teacher—Middle Childhood Generalist
Certified 2001/Renewed 2010

For information address Disney Press, 114 Fifth Avenue, New York, New York 10011-5690.

Visit www.disneybooks.com
Printed in China
ISBN 978-1-4231-6848-5
T425-2382-5-12153
First Edition
Written by Christina Wilsdon
Edited by Susan Bishansky
Fact-checked by Barbara Berliner
All rights reserved.

CONTENTS

WONDERFUL WORLD OF
DINOSAURS

AMAZING DINOSAURS!

Dinosaurs large and small dominated
the Earth for 135 million years!

GIANTS OF THE PAST

The world once belonged to dinosaurs—
amazing reptiles that could grow
to jaw-dropping sizes. Apatosaurus
was a giant plant-eater with a skyscraper
neck. Tyrannosaurus rex was a fierce
meat-eater with enormous teeth. Triceratops
had horns, and Ankylosaurus had skin
like armor. These awesome animals lived
alongside smaller dinosaurs, too. Chicken-
sized Compsognathus pecked up insects
and lizards for dinner.

Today, there are still animals that peck for food. Birds!
They are descended from a kind of dinosaur. So this means
that birds are dinosaurs, too!

GONE, BUT NOT FORGOTTEN

The first dinosaurs appeared about 230 million years ago.
Dinosaurs were the dominant life-form on land. No other land
animal has ever matched the size of the biggest dinosaurs.
About 65 million years ago, all the dinosaurs,
except for birds, died out. And just 200 years
ago, nobody even knew that dinosaurs had
ever existed!

Today, paleontologists—scientists who study
prehistoric life—continue to figure out how
these incredible animals lived. Every bone
they dig up is another piece in the dinosaur
puzzle. Sometimes, it even belongs to a new
kind of dinosaur!

HERE, THERE, SOMETIMES EVERYWHERE!

Some dinosaur species have been found in different parts of
the world. Other kinds seem to have lived in only a few places.
In dinosaur days, the continents were all close together.
Dinosaurs would have been able to travel over land in places
where modern land animals can't.

DINOSAURS UP CLOSE

There's more to a dinosaur than meets the eye! They might be big or small, ferocious or gentle, and have feathers, scales, or horns.

I'm *always* ready for my close-up!

T. rex, displayed here at Dinosaur Hall, Academy of Natural Sciences in Philadelphia, had 4-foot-long jaws!

Photo of T. rex display

Megalosaurus

Artist's rendering of Proterosuchus, a crocodile-like archosaur of the Early Triassic period

WHAT IS A
DINOSAUR?

They were **reptiles** that lived on land. They existed from about **230 million** years ago to **65 million** years ago. Like other reptiles, dinosaurs had clawed toes and laid eggs. They might have had scaly skin, fuzz, or feathers. What made them different from other reptiles? Dinosaurs stood with their legs *under* their bodies, not sprawled sideways like **lizards**.

ARE DINOSAURS RELATED TO
CROCODILES AND ALLIGATORS?

Yes—very distantly! The last ancestor they had in common was a reptile that lived more than 240 million years ago called an **archosaur**.

WHAT WAS
SPECIAL ABOUT ARCHOSAUR?

Archosaurs looked like other **reptiles**, but their skeletons showed changes, or adaptations. Their **ankle bones** worked like hinges, so it could also walk more upright instead of just sprawling. Also their teeth were rooted in sockets in their jaws. This would make their teeth less likely to fall out when eating. Dinosaurs and **crocodilians** (crocodiles, alligators, and their ancestors) show these features, too.

Archosaur

DINOSAURS AROUND THE WORLD

NORTH AMERICA

SOUTH AMERICA

Paleontologists find dino bones all over the world, from Antarctica to Zimbabwe! The western United States and Canada are a dinosaur gold mine! This huge area is wind-swept and weather-beaten. These conditions have uncovered ancient rocks containing dinosaur bones. People have been digging up dinosaurs there since the 1850s. In the past 20 years, dinosaur bits have surfaced in new places—South America, China, and Mongolia.

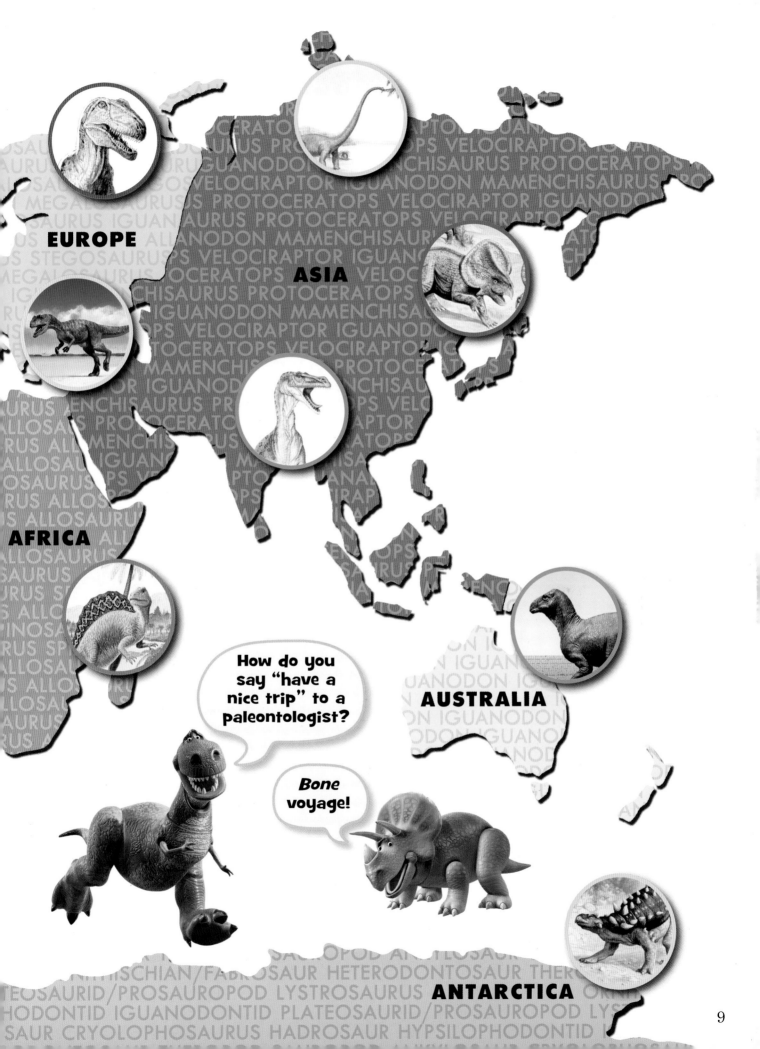

EUROPE

ASIA

AFRICA

AUSTRALIA

How do you say "have a nice trip" to a paleontologist?

Bone voyage!

ANTARCTICA

9

THE AGE OF DINOSAURS

Those were the good old days!

Dinosaurs ruled the world for hundreds of millions of years! Dino bones have been found in just about every part of the globe.

Most dinos didn't like to swim, but they didn't mind getting their feet wet.

Illustration of a group of Sauropods

Styracosaurus

Dimorphodon

WHAT IS THE
MESOZOIC?

The Mesozoic is a **span of time** in Earth's history—like a chapter. It started about 245 million years ago and ended 65 million years ago, when dinosaurs disappeared, or became **extinct**. Look at the timeline below. You can see that the Mesozoic is divided into three parts: the **Triassic**, the **Jurassic**, and the **Cretaceous**. Different dinosaurs lived during these three time periods. Herrerasaurus lived in the Triassic. Long-necked Apatosaurus lived during the Late Jurassic. Spiky Styracosaurus lived during the Late Cretaceous.

WHAT WAS THE
WORLD LIKE THEN?

Most of Earth's land was still just one big **continent** during the Triassic period. By the end of the Jurassic, it had **split** into two continents with a sea in between. The continents continued **drifting** apart during the Cretaceous, when the Atlantic Ocean formed.

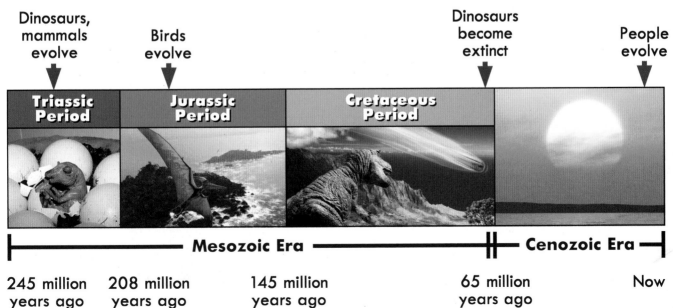

Dinosaurs, mammals evolve

Birds evolve

Dinosaurs become extinct

People evolve

Triassic Period	Jurassic Period	Cretaceous Period	

|← Mesozoic Era →|←| Cenozoic Era →|

| 245 million years ago | 208 million years ago | 145 million years ago | 65 million years ago | Now |

DINOSAUR NEIGHBORS

Dinosaurs weren't the only prehistoric animals! Some creatures even outlasted the dinos—right into the present day!

I remember some of these guys!

Quetzalcoatlus, one of the largest flying creatures ever, was named after a serpent god from Aztec mythology.

Model of a group of Quetzalcoatluses feeding on a carcass

WHAT OTHER ANIMALS LIVED ALONGSIDE DINOSAURS?

Wildlife in dinosaur times included insects, frogs and other amphibians, and reptiles large and small, including turtles, crocodilians, and flying reptiles called **pterosaurs**. Some of these prehistoric animals were big enough to eat even dinosaurs! "**SuperCroc**," for instance, was a 40-foot-long crocodilian that lived about 100 million years ago. It weighed about 8 tons—as much as a large African elephant!

"SuperCroc"

Ginkgo tree

Illustration of an ichthyosaur

WHAT ANIMALS LIVED IN THE SEA?

The oceans were jumping with **fish**. The first ones appeared about 500 million years ago, way before dinosaurs came along. There were shellfish (such as clams) and **corals**, too. The seas were also home to giant reptiles like the long-necked **plesiosaurs** and the sharklike ichthyosaurs. The first sea turtles, crabs, and lobsters appeared in the Jurassic.

WHAT PLANTS GREW DURING THE MESOZOIC?

Forests were filled with tall evergreen plants called **cycads**, as well as **ginkgo** trees. Conifers—cone-bearing trees such as pines— also sprouted up, as did ferns, brushy plants called **horsetails**, and scaly plants called **club mosses**. Some of these plants, such as horsetail and ginkgo, still grow today and look like their ancestors. They're called "**living fossils**."

DISCOVERING DINOSAURS

Dinosaur bones really puzzled people in the past! It took lots of work to make sense of such huge creatures!

I was discovered in a toy store!

Dicraeosaurus roamed what is now Africa in the Late Jurassic period.

Illustration of Dicraeosaurs

WHEN WERE DINOSAURS DISCOVERED?

People had been digging up dinosaur bones for centuries without knowing what they were. They came up with many explanations for these **bones**. Some thought the bones came from dragons, giant humans, or animals that lived inside rocks. Some even thought that the bones were put in the rocks by magic! In the **1820**s, scientist **William Buckland** dug up giant bones in **England**. By then, people realized that Earth was very old and that animals could become extinct.

Hylaeosaurus

Megalosaurus model by Richard Owen, as shown in Dinosaur Court, Crystal Palace, London, England

WHAT WERE THE FIRST DINOSAURS TO GET NAMES?

Buckland named the giant reptile he discovered **Megalosaurus**, which means "big lizard." He knew it was a big, meat-eating, land-dwelling reptile, and that it was different from other reptiles. In 1825, fossil-hunters Gideon and Mary Ann Mantell dug up a plant-eater that looked to them like a giant iguana. It's no surprise that they named it **Iguanodon**! In 1833, the Mantells uncovered spiky **Hylaeosaurus**, which means "forest lizard."

WHO CAME UP WITH THE WORD "DINOSAUR"?

British scientist **Richard Owen** did. He carefully studied three giant reptile fossils. He realized they had a lot in common. For one thing, they walked with their legs under their bodies. Other reptiles walked with their legs sprawled sideways. In 1842, he gave them the name "**Dinosauria**," which means "fearfully great lizards." In 1854, giant models of the dinosaurs went on display in **London**. To celebrate, Owen and about 20 guests had a dinner party inside one of them!

Sir Richard Owen

Guests dining inside a life-size model of Iguanodon at the Crystal Palace, London, December 31, 1853.

FOSSIL FACTS

Secrets of the prehistoric past are found in fossils. They hold the key to how far life on Earth has come!

In 1947, paleontologist Edwin H. Colbert found more than 1,000 fossilized skeletons of Coelophysis in a huge "grave" at New Mexico's Ghost Ranch.

Coelophysis fossil

Fossils of ginkgo tree

WHAT ARE FOSSILS?

Fossils are the **remains** of creatures that lived 10,000 years ago or more. The best known kinds of fossils are actual bones, teeth, claws, and shells. They are called "**body fossils**." Other fossils give clues about the activities of living things. These are called "**trace fossils**." Trace fossils include footprints, bite marks, droppings, and marks made by leaves, bark, feathers, skin, and even microscopic bacteria.

HOW DO DINO **BONES AND TEETH** BECOME FOSSILS?

A dead dinosaur would get **covered** by sand or mud over time. It might have been **buried** in an avalanche, caught in a flood, or **blanketed** by a sandstorm. Its soft parts would rot away. But its harder parts, such as bones and teeth, wouldn't. The mud or sand would eventually turn into rock and **preserve** the bones inside. Some or all of the bones might turn to stone, too. Water with minerals would seep into spaces in the bones. Then the minerals would harden and crystallize.

HOW DO PALEONTOLOGISTS FIGURE OUT **HOW OLD** A FOSSIL IS?

A fossil's age is linked to the **age of the rock** it's in. Scientists find out a rock's age by studying certain minerals that change over time into other minerals. Measuring how much the minerals changed is a clue to the rock's age. **Paleontologists** also look for fossils in the rock from other animals that lived during very specific time periods. Dinosaur fossils are probably the same age as these "**index fossils**" they're found with.

Tyrannosaurus rex skull

Dinosaur footprint

THE FIRST DINOSAURS

Fossils work like time machines to take us back to the age of the earliest dinosaurs.

I love looking at pictures of my great-great-great-great-great—well, lots of greats—grandparents!

Acrocanthosaurus was a 40-foot-long predator who was at the top of the food chain in what is now the American Southwest.

Photo of Acrocanthosaurus display at the North Carolina Museum of Natural Sciences

WERE ANY EARLY DINOSAURS REALLY BIG?

A 10-foot **Herrerasaurus** isn't exactly a tiny beast! But it's small compared to the giants most people imagine when they think of dinosaurs. The really huge dinosaurs didn't appear until the Jurassic, but the late Triassic had its big guys, such as **Antetonitrus**. This long-necked dinosaur weighed about **4,000 pounds** and was 33 feet long—about as long as a school bus. Its 215-million-year-old bones were unearthed in South Africa in 1981.

Herrerasaurus

Eoraptor running in the forest

WHAT DINOSAURS ARE THE OLDEST?

One of the oldest is **Herrerasaurus**, a 10-foot-long meat-eater. It ran on its hind legs and grabbed prey with three-clawed hands and long, sharp teeth. It may have eaten the 3-foot-long **Eoraptor**, another primitive dinosaur. Herrerasaurus lived during the Late Triassic. It shares only some features with other dinosaurs, so some **paleontologists** aren't sure if it is a true dino. Some think it may just be an ancient, dinosaurlike reptile that's only distantly related to dinosaurs.

Eoraptor

WHAT ANIMAL IS THE ANCESTOR OF ALL DINOSAURS?

The mother of all dinosaurs hasn't been found yet. But paleontologists have found many "**proto-dinosaurs**"— creatures a lot like dinosaurs. One, **Asilisaurus**, was discovered in 2007. It existed about 10 million years *before* Herrerasaurus. Other almost-but-not-quite dinos include the 3-foot-long predator **Marasuchus** and 5-foot-long plant-eater **Silesaurus**.

THAT'S REALLY
WILD!

A fossil find is often a jumble of bones from many dinosaurs—and early scientists often put together some very odd creatures!

Mix-and-match dinosaurs? What fun!

SWAMPED CHOMPERS

Scientists once thought that big, long-necked **plant-eaters** like **Apatosaurus** were so heavy, they couldn't have survived on land. They must have lived in **swamps**, where water could support them. By the 1970s, though, research showed that these dinosaurs actually did live on land. They not only held up their mighty tails, they also swung them in self-defense like giant clubs.

Apatosaurus

SKULLDUGGERY!

In 1879, **fossil-hunter** O.C. Marsh studied a shipment of dinosaur bones, then named the animal **Brontosaurus**. It didn't have a head, so he just slapped on a skull from another dinosaur fossil found somewhere else! In 1903, scientists pointed out that Marsh's Brontosaurus was really an **Apatosaurus**, which had been discovered two years before. In the 1970s, scientists also proved that Marsh had given his dino the skull of a **Camarasaurus**. Museums everywhere moved fast to replace their Apatosaurus noggins!

Apatosaurus (briefly known as Brontosaurus)

Iguanodon

THAT'S A
NO-NOSE

British scientist Gideon Mantell goofed when he first tried to piece together **Iguanodon**. He put bones from its rear end into its shoulders, gave it sprawling, lizardlike legs, and stuck a **horn** on its nose! Later scientists figured out that the nose horn was actually a **thumb**!

KINDS OF DINOSAURS

I'm a *kind* kind of dinosaur.

Like modern animals, dinosaurs were of many kinds, or species. And the list grows with each new discovery.

Diplodocus is one of the most recognizable dinosaurs.

Model of Diplodocus

HOW MANY SPECIES OF DINOSAURS ARE THERE?

Paleontologists have found around **600 species**. About half are known from only a handful of bones. As new fossils are **discovered**, the number of species grows. Every year, about 15 new species are identified. But these "new" dinosaurs don't always pop up while digging outdoors. **Paleontologists** also find them by studying old fossils. They give them a fresh look using new information.

A herd of Apatosauruses

WHAT'S THE DIFFERENCE BETWEEN THE TWO MAIN DINO GROUPS?

Dinosaurs are divided into groups just as modern animals are. The two main groups are **Saurischia** ("lizard-hipped") and **Ornithischia** ("bird-hipped"). Saurischian dinos like Apatosaurus and Tyrannosaurus rex had **hip** structures a lot like a lizard's. Ornithischians like Stegosaurus, Ankylosaurus, and Triceratops had hip structures that were more like a bird's. Saurischians also might have had hands with a **thumb**. That thumb was often tipped with a large **claw**. These dinos were also known for their long necks.

Stegosaurus

Tyrannosaurus rex

WHAT **BIG TEETH** YOU HAVE!

Carnosaurs were saurischian dinosaurs with *big* appetites.

The carnosaur *Allosaurus* is Utah's official state fossil!

Smaller herbivores like Dryosaurus didn't stand a chance against a hungry Allosaurus!

Illustration of Allosaurus chasing Dryosaurs

WHAT IS A CARNOSAUR?

"Carnosaur" means "**meat-eating lizard**." Everything about a carnosaur shows it was built to hunt, kill, and **devour**! A carnosaur usually had a hatchetlike skull, strong forearms, long claws, and teeth like steak knives.

Allosaurus

Allosaurus

WHAT ARE SOME OTHER CARNOSAURS?

Allosaurus's cousins include one of the biggest meat-eating dinosaurs ever, **Giganotosaurus**. At **46 feet**, it was a little bit longer than Allosaurus, but it was twice as heavy. Acrocanthosaurus is famous for the big **spines** running down its back.

WHAT IS THE BEST-KNOWN CARNOSAUR?

Fossil hunters have found many bones from **Allosaurus**. This Late Jurassic carnosaur grew to 30 to **40 feet long**. Its head alone measured about 3 feet! The head had bony ridges on top and two short horns above the eyes. Its teeth were up to 4 inches long! Scientists aren't sure how Allosaurus got food, though. It may have been a **scavenger**, eating dead animals it didn't kill. Its tooth marks were found on the bones of Apatosaurus. Or it may have been a hunter. Dinosaur footprints found in Texas show Allosaurus tracks running alongside prints made by the giant dinosaur **Sauroposeidon**. Allosaurus may have hunted in packs, like wolves.

Acrocanthosaurus

Giganotosaurus

TYRANT DINOS ON THE LOOSE

Tyrant dinosaurs were fierce hunters. They ate their way through bones, armor skin, and even spikes!

Meet my cousins, aunts, and uncles!

Tyrants like T. rex are as scary to us today as they were to animals of their age.

Illustration of T. rex hunting Ornithomimus

WHAT'S A
TYRANT
DINOSAUR?

Tyrant dinosaurs, like carnosaurs, were **theropods**. This means they were saurischian—"lizard-hipped"—and walked on their **hind legs**. The tyrants had big heads, short forearms, and strong jaws. Their eyes looked more forward than other theropods' eyes did. This helped them see like a modern predator, such as a lion or wolf. Tyrant dinosaurs also had sharp, thick, **spiky teeth** that delivered a bone-crushing bite. **Daspletosaurus** was one hefty tyrant. Gorgosaurus was a lighter and smaller model.

WHAT DID
TYRANNOSAURUS REX
EAT?

Anything it wanted! T. rex probably ate other dinosaurs such as horned **Triceratops**, duck-billed Edmontosaurus, and ostrichlike theropods. Sometimes it even crushed and swallowed **bones** as it gobbled its meal. Bite marks on Tyrannosaurus rex bones show that these fierce **predators** may even have eaten each other! Like lions today, however, T. rex was also happy to scavenge.

WHAT'S THE
MOST FAMOUS
TYRANT DINOSAUR?

Meet **Tyrannosaurus rex**! This dinosaur's name means "king of the tyrant lizards"—and for good reason! T. rex lived during the Late Cretaceous. It weighed about 7 tons and stood about **20 feet tall**! T. rex relied on its banana-size teeth to rip apart prey, then gulp it down in 500-pound chunks. Struggling victims had no chance of escaping the claws on its **two-fingered hands**!

Tyrannosaurus rex

RAPID RAPTORS

Yikes! Watch out for these dinos!

The "raptor dinosaurs" were running razorblades— with feathers!

Raptors didn't care if their prey was bigger than they were!

Model of Deinonychosaurs stalking Iguanodon

WHAT'S A
RAPTOR
DINOSAUR?

"Raptor," in dino-speak, is a nickname for the **Deinonychosaurs**— the "fearsome **claw lizards**." And fearsome they were! Like other theropods, they ran on their hind legs. Each back foot had a large, curved claw that was held up off the ground. They had long, **flexible arms** and three-clawed hands that gripped prey and tore it apart. In 1971, researchers in Mongolia dug up a plant-eating dinosaur called **Protoceratops**. It must have been battling with a Velociraptor because one of the raptor's claws was still stuck in its neck!

WAS VELOCIRAPTOR
SMART?

Velociraptor had a **brain** that was large for its body size. The same goes for raptors such as Troodon and Bambiraptor. Animals whose brains are large for their body size tend to be more **intelligent**, so these raptors were probably pretty **clever**.

Velociraptors

HOW DO WE KNOW VELOCIRAPTORS MAY HAVE HAD
FEATHERS?

Velociraptor arm bones have bumps like the ones on bird **wing bones** that show where feathers were attached. Most paleontologists think this is a sign that **Velociraptor** and other raptors had feathers, too. The dinosaurs didn't fly, but feathers may have kept them warm, attracted mates, or **propelled** some of them as they ran up tree trunks flapping their arms.

Deinonychus hand

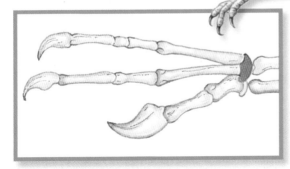

Deinonychus

29

SUPERSIZED
SAUROPODS

Munching on trees was a breeze for these long-necked legends! The only thing "small" about them was their brain!

I wonder what the weather's like up there!

Sauropods were giants even though they weren't meat-eaters!

Model of Sauropod

WHAT IS A
SAUROPOD?

A sauropod had a **very long neck**, a small head, and legs like an elephant's. Many sauropods also had really **long tails**. They walked on all fours, though some species may have been able to rear up on their hind legs. **Sauropods** lived from the Late Triassic to the end of the Cretaceous, when dinosaurs went extinct.

Sauropods eating leaves

Brachiosaurus

Apatosaurus (Brontosaurus)

WHY DID SAUROPODS HAVE
LONG NECKS?

Sauropods probably used them to **reach leaves** high up on trees. They may also have swept their heads from side to side to munch on low-growing bushes. Sauropods had big, heavy bodies. **Grazing** this way would have saved them **energy**.

WHAT SAUROPOD HAD THE
LONGEST NECK?

The longest known neck compared to body size belongs to **Mamenchisaurus**. This dinosaur, found in China, was at least **85 feet long** from nose to tail. Its neck made up nearly half its length!

Mamenchisaurus

APATOSAURUS
AND COMPANY

Sauropods came in many sizes, including extra-extra-large! They were some of the biggest creatures to ever walk the Earth.

These guys really stuck their necks out!

Apatosaurus, one of the biggest animals ever, weighed as much as four elephants!

Model of Apatosaurus

WHAT SAUROPODS HAVE I HEADR OF?

Apatosaurus is one of the most famous dinosaurs ever. Its fossils were dug up in the late 1800s, making Apatosaurus one of the first sauropods to be discovered. It measured about 75 feet long and weighed about 30 tons. **Diplodocus** was slimmer and longer. **Brachiosaurus** was a 50-ton sauropod with extra-long front legs. It was as tall as a five-story building!

Brachiosaurus

Diplodocus

WHAT ELSE WAS SPECIAL ABOUT THEM?

Apatosaurus and Diplodocus had long tails that ended in a thin, **flexible whip**. These sauropods probably used their tails as **weapons** to slash Allosaurus and other predators. The tails may have **snapped** faster than the speed of sound, creating a loud bang—a **sonic boom**! Sauropods did not have teeth shaped for chewing. Brachiosaurus probably ate hundreds of pounds of leaves a day. That food probably slowly stewed in its **vat-like body** with the help of bacteria—the same way cows digest their food.

WHAT WAS THE BIGGEST SAUROPOD?

Argentinosaurus currently holds the record. It may have spanned 130 feet or more! It probably weighed in at **90 tons**. Another dinosaur may one day claim the title, though. **Sauroposeidon** is known from just a few bones. But a few of them are neck bones measuring 4 feet long apiece!

Argentinosaurus

33

THAT'S REALLY WILL!

Edmontosaurus

I'm the *friendliest* dinosaur!

WHO'S BIGGEST?
WHO'S SMALLEST?

The answers change often as we learn more about dinosaurs. For now, these are some of the superstars.

Shantungosaurus

THE TOOTHIEST DINOSAUR

The award for most teeth goes to **Shantungosaurus**, a 50-foot-long plant-eater from the Late Cretaceous. It was a kind of dinosaur called a **hadrosaur**—its teeth were designed to grind up tough plants. Shantungosaurus did the job with **1,500 teeth**. Most were packed together to act as a shredder. The rest were tucked away as backups for worn-out teeth.

Lambeosaurus skull

Spinosaurus

THE **BIGGEST**
MEAT-EATING DINO

T. rex was big. Giganotosaurus was even bigger. But biggest of all the meat-eaters, or carnivores, was Spinosaurus. **Spinosaurus** weighed about 8 tons and reached about **52 feet long**. It had long, crocodile-like jaws for seizing other dinosaurs and big fish. Spinosaurus is named for the long **spines** on its back.

Spinosaurus skeleton on display in Paris

Spinosaurus hunting other dinosaurs

THE SMALLEST DINOSAUR

Not all dinosaurs were huge. Some were no bigger than a chicken! The smallest known so far is the Ashdown maniraptoran. This **birdlike** dinosaur walked on its hind legs and had a long neck and a short tail. It was about a foot long and weighed about as much as a banana. One little guy, **Micropachycephalosaurus**, may also have stood only a foot high. But it wins the award for longest dino name. The 23-letter word means "small, thick-headed lizard."

Maniraptoran

35

DINOSAURS IN ARMOR

The days of the dinosaur were dangerous. Wearing armor was one way to play it safe in the Mesozoic!

I have spears. These guys had shields!

Even Euoplocephalus' eyelids were made of bony armor!

Model of Euoplocephaluses

WHAT WAS DINO ARMOR MADE OF?

Armored dinosaurs were **protected** by bony plates in their skins called **osteoderms**. "Osteo" means "bone," and derm means "skin." And that's exactly what osteoderms are: **skin bones**. These slabs of bone are part of the skin, like bony **freckles**. Today's crocodiles, alligators, lizards, and armadillos all wear a similar coat of armor.

Three Ankylosauruses fighting with Albertosaurus

Struthiosaurus

WHO HAD THE HEAVIEST ARMOR?

Ankylosaurs. These plant-eaters were built like **tanks**! They lived from the middle of the Jurassic to the end of the Cretaceous. Edmontonia and Gastonia bristled with **huge spikes**. Ankylosaurus had armor plus a tail that ended in a ball made of fused osteoderms. Any predator that dared to attack Ankylosaurus risked being bashed by this heavy, **spiked club**!

HOW BIG WAS THE LARGEST OSTEODERM?

Paleontologists found a a **22-inch-long** osteoderm slab from a sauropod. But it's mostly hollow inside, so it wasn't very strong. These osteoderms may have been storehouses for **minerals** that a dinosaur needed but couldn't always find in its food. The minerals may have been absorbed by the dinosaur's body to keep its bones strong or to help it lay eggs that had **strong shells**.

Ankylosaurus

STEGOSAURS:
SPIKES AND PLATES

These dinosaurs always had a "back-up" plan. They were like walking weapons!

I'd love to have a spike or two!

Stegosaurus may have had a big body, but its brain was only about as big as a walnut!

Illustration of Stegosaurus

Stegosaurus

WHAT WERE
STEGOSAURS?

They were plant-eaters from the middle Jurassic to the Late Cretaceous. These armored animals are known as "**plated dinosaurs**." The "plates" are tall slabs that stick up from a stegosaur's **backbone**. In some species, the slabs were spikes. All stegosaurs had **spiky tails** that they used as weapons.

Fossilized skeleton of Stegosaurus

WHAT WERE THE
PLATES FOR?

When you think of spikes and armor, you think of **weapons**. But paleontologists have a harder time explaining the flat plates. They first thought the plates lay flat, like paving stones, instead of standing upright. Stegosaurs may have used them to **heat up** and **cool down**. Or maybe they helped species of stegosaurs recognize each other or **attract mates**.

DID STEGOSAURUS REALLY HAVE
TWO BRAINS?

Stegosaurus is the most **popular** plated dino. It's also been in the middle of many mix-ups, such as the "**two-brain**" story. Like any other animal, Stegosaurus had just one brain, located in its head. The idea that it had a second brain in its **backside** got started in the late 1800s. A scientist found a big space in Stegosaurus's backbone. He thought it may have held a bundle of **nerves**—like a brain— that controlled the tail.

BEAKY BEASTS

These plant eaters were the cows of their time. The world was their pasture!

They like the same food I do!

All ornithopods like Hadrosaurus were plant-eaters that stood on two feet.

Illustration of Hadrosaurs

WHAT IS AN ORNITHOPOD?

"Ornithopod" means "**bird feet**." This name came about because scientists in the late 1800s thought the **hind feet** looked like a bird's. An ornithopod was even more birdlike up front. Its snout ended in a tough, **sharp beak**.

Ornithopod

Iguanodon

WHAT DID THEY **EAT?**

Ornithopods ate **plants**. Their beaks easily **cut leaves** and twigs from plants. They had lots of strong teeth made for **grinding**. They had the most teeth of any dinosaur—hundreds of them! Ornithopods could move their jaws to chew. Most other dinosaurs could only swallow food in chunks or, at best, crunch it a little.

WHAT ARE SOME ORNITHOPODS I MIGHT KNOW?

Iguanodon was one of the first dinosaur fossils ever **discovered**. At first, people thought it looked like a **giant iguana**. It didn't! It walked on all fours but could also stand on its hind legs. Its thumbs were **huge spikes**. Iguanodon was up to 33 feet long and lived in the early Cretaceous. **Ouranosaurus** and **Dollodon** had tall spines on their backs. **Altirhinus** had a huge, arched snout, so it probably had a big, bulbous nose, too.

Iguanodon

Ouranosaurus

MEET THE DUCKBILLS

Some dinosaurs had bills like a duck. Paleontologists call these duck-billed dinos "hadrosaurs."

Duckbills always *quack* me up!

Hadrosaurids were the largest of the duckbills.

Photo of duckbill display

Parasaurolophus
skull

WHAT DUCKBILLS HAD
CRESTS
ON THEIR HEADS?

The amazing-looking **lambeosaurines** had hollow, bony crests on the tops of their heads. Lambeosaurus had a hatchet-shaped crest. **Parasaurolophus** had a long, hollow tube that curved over its neck. The crest contained tubes that linked to the duckbill's **nostrils**. Early paleontologists thought duckbills lived in water. The crests would act like **snorkels** to keep water out of the lungs. But now we know that duckbills lived on land. The crest probably worked as an **"echo chamber"** so the animal could honk or grunt loudly.

WHAT IS A
DUCKBILL?

Like Iguanodon, duckbills were ornithopods. Their **beaks** looked more like a duck's bill, though, because their **snouts** were **wide** and **curved**. Many duckbills also had hundreds of teeth for grinding up leaves and twigs. Duckbills didn't have spiky thumbs like their ornithopod cousins did.

Lambeosaurus

HOW **BIG**
WERE DUCKBILLS?

Pararhabdodon was half as long as a bus and weighed as much as a horse. Not small! But **Shantungosaurus** was gigantic at 50 feet long and possibly **13 tons**. That's as much as two elephants! Shantungosaurus may have been the largest animal to ever walk on its hind legs.

Corythosauruses

BONEHEADS

The pachycephalosaurs had built-in helmets. Talk about "hard-headed"!

These guys really *were* boneheads!

Scientists are still scratching their heads about why these dinos had such thick skulls. Was it for ramming each other or for recognizing each other?

Illustration of two Pachycephalosaurs

Two pachycephalosaurs doing battle

WHAT'S A
PACHYCEPHALOSAUR?

"Pachycephalosaur" means "**thick-headed reptile**." These dinosaurs had very thick skulls—six inches or more of bone to protect a tiny brain! Pachycephalosaurus also had spikes on the back of its head and on its nose. **Stygimoloch** had two 6-inch-long **spikes** and several smaller ones sticking out of its head. These "**boneheads**" all walked on their hind legs.

WHY WERE THEIR HEADS
SO HARD?

Many paleontologists think that male pachycephalosaurs used their bony heads to **ram** other males in fights for mates. They probably didn't smack their heads together, though. They most likely just **pushed** each other around, like deer. Some fossils have big **bumps of bone**, and others have smaller bumps. Maybe this means that males and females had different head shapes, just as some species do today.

Stygimoloch

WERE PACHYCEPHALOSAURS
FEROCIOUS?

To each other, maybe! They were **plant-eaters**, so they didn't prey on other dinosaurs. They weren't very big, either. **Stenopelix** stood at 4.5 feet, and Pachycephalosaurus reached 15 feet.

Stenopelix

FRILLS, SPIKES, AND HORNS!

No other dinosaur headgear matched that of the ceratopsians. They went everywhere in style!

Now these are *my* kind of dinos!

Triceratops, at up to 30 feet long, was probably the biggest ceratopsian.

Model of Triceratops

WHAT IS A CERATOPSIAN?

"Ceratopsian" means "**horn-faced**." This group of plant-eaters is named for the many species with horns on their heads—and often their **noses**, too! But some ceratopsians of the early Cretaceous, like **Psittacosaurus**, didn't have any horns at all. Some were big, like the 29-foot **Triceratops**. And others were small. **Bagaceratops** was only as long as a yardstick! What all ceratopsians had in common was a bone at the tip of the upper jaw. No other dinosaurs had it.

Triceratops skull

Psittacosaurus skull

WHAT IS A TRICERATOPS?

Triceratops, the most popular ceratopsian, is famous for the **two horns** above its eyes, the big horn on its nose, and the **bony frill** flaring over its neck. Centrosaurus showed off a spiky frill and dagger-shaped horn. And the frill of **Styracosaurus** had so many spikes, it looked like a giant buzz saw!

Triceratops

WHAT'S WITH THE FRILLS?

Some ceratopsians had frills made of solid bone. This made scientists think the frills might have worked as **shields** to protect their necks from predators. But other species had frills with big spaces in them that would have been covered only with skin. That's why paleontologists now think the frills were used mostly for **communicating** with other ceratopsians. Colors and patterns on the frills might also have helped males and females **identify** others of their species.

Styracosaurus

THAT'S REALLY WILD!

I have some pretty amazing relatives!

Therizinosaurus

Mononykus

ANT-OSAURUS?

Mononykus was a goose-size dinosaur with **long legs** and very short, powerful arms. Each arm ended in just one big claw. This claw may have been used to rip open the nests of ants and termites. Mononykus would then gobble them all up in its **beaky** mouth.

EGGS-PLAIN THE NAMES!

Oviraptor means "**egg thief**." The six-foot theropod got this name in the 1920s when a fossil skull was found with fossil eggs. Researchers assumed Oviraptor was raiding a nest! Later finds led them to believe it was protecting the nest. **Deinocheirus**'s name means "**horrible hand**." This dino had 8-foot-long arms, each ending in a set of three 8-inch-long claws! **Therizinosaurus** sported 3-foot-long claws on its hands— the **biggest claws** of any animal, ever!

Oviraptor

Deinonychus

Lexovisaurus

LOOKING SHARP!

Lexovisaurus had a **spiky tail**, like other stegosaurs. It also had two giant spikes that stuck out sideways from its shoulders. Some paleontologists think the **spines** might have been on its hips, though.

BABY DINOSAURS

Dinosaurs hatched from eggs. Like the dinos themselves, the eggs came in all sizes and shapes.

All dinosaurs laid eggs, but not all of them were good parents! Scientists are still trying to figure out what dino family life was like.

Model of Maiasaur eggs hatching

Maiasaura nesting grounds

DID DINOSAURS **CARE** FOR THEIR EGGS?

Many probably did—but not all. Scientists have found fossil eggs arranged in **circles** and **spirals**. This is a clue that one or both parents took care of the eggs, carefully moving them after they were laid. Paleontologists have even found fossils of dinosaurs **protecting** their eggs! In 1995, researchers discovered a fossilized Citipati **huddling** over a batch of eggs.

Protoceratops nest and eggs

DID DINOSAURS CARE FOR THEIR **BABIES?**

Exciting finds may lead to new ideas about how dinosaur babies grew up. Nobody thought dinosaurs cared for their young until 1978. Paleontologists discovered **fossilized Maiasaura** babies and eggs in Montana. They also found **nests** and fossil plant material. These fossils showed that these duckbill **hatchlings** may have stayed in the nest and were fed there by their parents. In 2004, researchers found a fossil **Psittacosaurus** in a nest with 34 babies, and in 2011 they found a nest with 15 Protoceratops babies.

WHAT DID DINOSAUR EGGS **LOOK LIKE?**

Dinosaur eggs had hard shells like bird eggs. Some eggs were **round**, while others were shaped more like **potatoes**. They might have been smaller than a chicken's, or a **foot long**, like the eggs of the sauropod Hypselosaurus. The duckbill Hypacrosaurus laid round eggs the size of **bowling balls**!

A DINOSAUR GROWS UP

Dino bones tell the story of how they grew up. If dinosaurs had worn shoes, they'd have outgrown them every week!

Scientists can get clues to how long dinosaurs like Styracosaurus lived by looking at related animals of today. One, the tortoise, can live for more than 150 years!

Illustration of Styracosaurs

HOW **LONG** DID IT TAKE FOR A DINOSAUR TO **GROW UP?**

Triceratops with young

Most dino babies grew up **quickly**. Small species were adults by age **2 or 3**. Duckbills were fully grown by age **7 or 8**. Tyrannosaurus grew more slowly. It would have a growth spurt at about 10 and reach **full size** by age 20. Amazingly, even tiny sauropod babies small enough to perch on their mother's toes grew into giants in less than 20 years.

HOW DO PALEONTOLOGISTS FIGURE OUT A DINO'S **AGE?**

They use high-powered **microscopes** to examine the insides of dinosaur bones. The structure of a bone contains the history of how an animal grew. Many bones have layers of growth called **bone rings**. Each ring marks one year of growth, like tree rings. Other species don't have rings. This hints that they grew quickly, without spurts, like **T. rex**. Researchers then compare this information with what we know about how modern animals grow.

Museum technician reliefing a fossil bone

Dinosaur fossil

HOW LONG DID DINOSAURS LIVE?

Most paleontologists think T. rex and other big theropod predators didn't live past **age 30**. Ceratopsians and duckbills may have lived for 10 to 20 years. Apatosaurus and other sauropods might have lived to between **age 50** and **100**. Some scientists used to think dinos could live up to **300 years**!

THE AGE OF DINOSAURS ENDS

I'm glad I'm not extinct!

About 65 million years ago, all the dinosaurs (except birds) disappeared, along with half of all other living things.

No one knows yet why birds didn't go extinct with the dinosaurs.

Model of asteroid approaching Earth's surface

WHY DID DINOSAURS GO EXTINCT?

The most widely accepted theory for their disappearance is that an **asteroid** slammed into Earth. In the 1970s, scientists tested a layer of clay found in more than 100 places worldwide. It had a lot of an **element** that's rare on Earth but common in space. This meant that an asteroid had crashed into Earth. Then, in 1981, a 112-mile-wide **crater** was discovered under the sea off Mexico. Specks of asteroid and other clues there also make this idea a possibility.

HOW COULD AN ASTEROID WIPE OUT DINOSAURS?

The asteroid would have caused a huge **explosion**. Dust and ash shot into the atmosphere worldwide would have blocked out sunlight. The Earth would become dark and cold. The crash would also have caused **earthquakes** and giant ocean waves called **tsunamis**. Acid rain would fall. Then, high levels of carbon dioxide would bring on **global warming**. You can see how such a disaster would shake up life on Earth!

WHAT OTHER ANIMALS DISAPPEARED WHEN THE DINOS DID?

Living things large and small died out, down to many kinds of **plankton**—tiny sea creatures. Plesiosaurs and other ocean **reptiles** went extinct. Many **mammals** died out, too. Insects, many land reptiles and mammals, and many birds made it through. No one knows why birds are the only dinosaurs that survived.

Meteorite falling to Earth

DINOSAURS, BIRDS, AND DINO-BIRDS

Believe it or not, dinosaurs may still roam the Earth today—in the form of birds.

One of my best friends is a canary-osaurus!

Pteranodon was one of the largest known flying reptiles!

Illustration of Pteranodon

ARE **BIRDS** DINOSAURS?

Most scientists agree that birds are dinosaurs. Birds are **avian** dinosaurs ("avian" means "**of birds**"). Apatosaurus, Triceratops, and other dinos large and small are non-avian dinosaurs.

Archaeopteryx

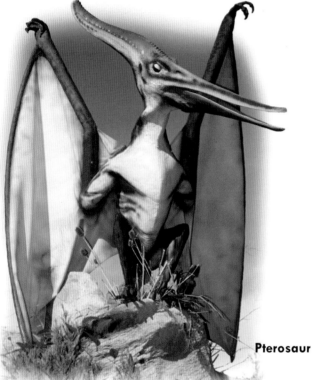

Pterosaur

WHAT IS **ARCHAEOPTERYX?**

Archaeopteryx is either a **birdlike** dinosaur or a dinosaurlike bird! For more than a hundred years, it was thought to be the **first bird**. But because of new discoveries, we're not sure anymore of Archaeopteryx's place in the bird family tree. In 2011, Chinese paleontologist **Xing Xu** wrote about Xiaotingia, a **pigeon-size** creature similar to Archaeopteryx. Some paleontologists think both animals may be dinosaurs, not early birds. If true, then Archaeopteryx may not have been the "early bird" after all!

WHEN DID PEOPLE FIRST SUSPECT THAT **BIRDS** ARE **DINOSAURS?**

Scientists have noticed how much birds have in **common** with two-legged, meat-eating dinos since the late 1800s. In 1861, a fossil that looked like a **cross** between a bird and a reptile was discovered in Germany. The 150-million-year-old creature had clawed **fingers**, a long, bony tail, teeth, and traces of **feathers** around its arms and tail. This fossil belongs to Archaeopteryx, which means "**ancient wing**."

Pterodactylus

LOOKING FOR EARLY BIRDS

Paleontologists are working to piece together the puzzle of bird history.

Gee, I would've liked having feathers.

Ornithocheirus had the wingspan of a small plane. Was it a bird, a dinosaur—or both?

Illustration of Ornithocheirus in flight

WHAT **KIND** OF DINOSAUR IS A BIRD?

Paleontologists think birds came from a **feathery** dinosaur called a **coelurosaurian**. A coelurosaurian wasn't just one species of dinosaur. Coelurosaurians were a big group that split off into many other groups—including tyrannosaurs!

Sinornithosaurus

Anurognathus

Protarchaeopteryx robusta

WHAT CLUES SEPARATE EARLY BIRDS FROM **NON-AVIAN** DINOS?

Paleontologists don't just look for feathers. They also study clues in the **skeletons**. They look for long arms, clawed fingers, specialized **wrist** bones, and other bony structures that might mean a fossil is a bird relative. Fossils of both early birds and **non-avian** dinos have clues about dinosaur and bird history, how feathers evolved, and how and when birds began to fly.

DID NON-AVIAN DINOSAURS HAVE **FEATHERS?**

Most dinosaur "feathers" are fluffy, fuzzy, or **hairy** structures called **protofeathers**. Protofeathers may have helped a dinosaur stay warm or find a mate. Some dinosaurs had feathers much like a modern bird's.

Pterodactylus

59

BRINGING DINOSAURS TO LIFE

Great fossil finds have helped us identify many kinds of dinosaurs. There's always more to learn from new discoveries—and old ones, too!

Look alive, dinos!

Dinosaur displays give a good idea of just how giant, or long-necked, or boneheaded these ancient creatures were.

Dinosaur display at the Children's Museum of Indianapolis, Indianapolis, Indiana

ARE THERE STILL MORE DINOS TO DISCOVER?

New dinosaur species are being dug up all the time. In 2009, paleontologists introduced **Miragaia**, a stegosaur with an extra-long neck. **Brontomerus**, a sauropod that may have defended itself by kicking predators, joined the pack in **2011**.

Fossil skeleton of Heterodontosaurus in clay

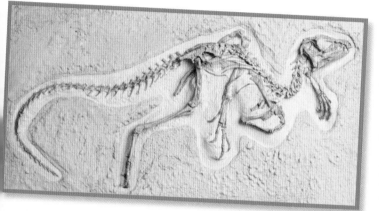

DO PALEONTOLOGISTS STUDY ONLY NEW FOSSILS?

It's exciting to find new dinosaur bones! But old fossils still have **secrets** for us to unleash. As technology improves, these "old" sources can give up new information. One **machine** lets us now see what's inside a bone without breaking it open. Sometimes, a new species is discovered by taking a fresh look at old fossils. This happened in **2004**, when scientists at a London museum found a new ceratopsian tucked away in a storeroom! **Spinops** had been sitting on a shelf since **1916**!

Teeth of a Tyrannosaurus rex fossil

WHAT ELSE CAN FOSSILS TELL US ABOUT DINOSAURS?

We may soon be able to figure out what **colors** dinosaurs were! In 2010, microscopic color-containing specks were found in Sinosauropteryx feathers and fuzz. Another team of scientists used this information to "**paint**" the full body color of a chicken-size dinosaur called Anchiornis. This black, gray, orange, and white animal is the first dinosaur to be revealed in its true colors! We may someday know how dinosaurs **acted** and how their bodies worked. Were they **warm-blooded** or **cold-blooded**? How fast did they move? Maybe someday you'll be the scientist who helps answer questions like these!

Plumage (feathers) show in fossil of a young Sinosauropteryx

GLOSSARY

Archosaur: Triassic reptiles that included dinosaurs, crocodilians, and pterosaurs

Avian dinosaurs: birds

Carnivore: an animal that eats meat

Cretaceous: The third and last period of the Mesozoic era

Crocodilian: crocodiles, alligators, and their ancestors

Dinosaur: extinct reptiles that lived on land

Duckbills: plant-eating dinosaurs with ducklike bills; also called hadrosaurs

Extinct: no longer in existence

Fossil: remains of an organism that died 10,000 years ago or more

Jurassic: the second of the three periods of the Mesozoic era

Mesozoic: a period of time in Earth's history that lasted from 245 million years ago to 65 million years ago

Non-avian dinosaurs: all dinosaurs that are not birds

Ornithischia: the "bird-hipped" dinosaurs

Osteoderm: a slab of bone embedded in skin

Paleontologist: a scientist who studies prehistoric life

Predator: an animal that eats other animals

Prey: an animal eaten by another animal

Proto-dinosaur: a closely related ancestor of the dinosaurs

Protofeathers: feather-like skin structures that came before the evolution of true feathers

Reptile: an animal group that includes dinosaurs, crocodilians, lizards, turtles, snakes, and their ancestors

Saurischia: the "lizard-hipped" dinosaurs

Sauropod: large, plant-eating dinosaurs that walked on all fours

Scavenging: feeding on carcasses of prey killed by other animals

Species: kinds of living things

Theropod: saurischian dinosaurs that walked on their hind legs and ate mostly meat

Triassic: the first of the three periods of the Mesozoic era

INDEX

PHOTO CREDITS